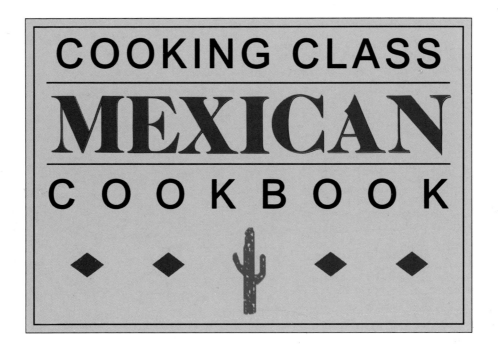

COOKING CLASS

MEXICAN

COOKBOOK

PUBLICATIONS INTERNATIONAL, LTD.

ISBN: 1-56173-985-5

Pictured on the front cover: Cheese & Chorizo Burritos (*page 14*).
Pictured on the inside front cover: Baked Shrimp with Chili-Garlic Butter (*page 70*).
Pictured on the back cover: Chicken Enchiladas (*page 26*).

8 7 6 5 4 3 2 1

Manufactured in the U.S.A.

CONTENTS

Nachos Olé (page 12)

Pork Burritos (page 40)

Zesty Zucchini-Chick Pea Salad (page 78)

CLASS NOTES

Tacos, burritos, enchiladas – once considered exotic foods, they are now as familiar as earlier imports of pizza, quiche and egg rolls. Due to their vibrant flavors, enticing textural contrasts and eye-catching colors these Mexican dishes have been readily accepted into our menus.

Mexican cuisine is more diverse than the taco lover might suspect. Based on foods such as corn, tomatoes, chilies and beans, this cuisine has developed over centuries and was shaped by unique geography, climate, indigenous foods and the native Indian culture. Mexican cuisine was also enhanced, but not overshadowed, by the Spanish introduction of their cooking techniques and domestic animals.

The recipes in this book were chosen to illustrate the variety of this wonderful cuisine; they range from subtle to spicy, simple to complex, rustic to sophisticated. Using authentic ingredients and cooking techniques, and presented with clear instructions and how-to photos, these dishes are sure to be a success even to the novice cook.

EQUIPMENT

Mexican cuisine requires very little in the way of specialized equipment, but a few items call for some discussion.

Bean Masher: A solid wooden block or perforated metal disk attached to a handle, this tool is very useful for the proper stirring and mashing needed to make refried beans. If necessary, a potato masher can be substituted.

Mortar and Pestle: Used to grind whole spices, herbs and nuts into a powder. The mortar is a bowl-shaped container and the pestle is a rounded-bottomed utensil. The mortar and pestle come as a set and are made out of marble, hardwood, porcelain or stoneware.

Spice or Coffee Grinder, Electric: A small appliance that effectively and quickly grinds whole spices. It can be used to prepare pure fresh chili powder from whole dried chilies. It is also used to grind seeds and nuts into the fine powder that is needed for some sauces, a function neither the blender nor food processor performs as well.

Tortilla Press: The press consists of two flat metal disks (usually 6 inches in diameter) that are hinged on one side and have a pressing handle attached at the opposite side. It is inexpensive and readily available in cookware shops and Mexican markets. A tortilla press is essential for speed and accuracy if you plan to make corn tortillas on a regular basis. However, you can improvise pressing the dough with the bottom of a heavy skillet or pie plate.

MEXICAN INGREDIENTS

These ingredients are normally available in Mexican groceries. Many can be found in supermarkets and gourmet food stores and some can be purchased in other Latin American, Caribbean and even Oriental food stores.

Annatto Seeds (also called achiote): Small, hard crimson-colored seeds used primarily in the Mayan-based cooking of the Yucatan. The seeds impart a deep yellow color and mild but distinctive flavor. They are soaked to soften or ground to a fine powder before using.

Chayote: A pear-shaped, pale green, soft-skinned squash with a delicious delicate flavor. It is also called mirliton or christophene. Chayote is generally available in the winter months and can be eaten raw, sautéed or baked. Store it in a plastic bag in the refrigerator for up to one month.

Chilies: See the descriptions on pages 7–8.

Chorizo: An orange- or red-colored, coarse-textured pork sausage sold bulk-style or stuffed into casings. The flavor ranges from highly seasoned to quite hot. Always remove the casing before using.

Cilantro (also called fresh coriander or Chinese parsley): A pungent herb with green delicate leaves, similar in appearance, but not flavor, to flat-leaf parsley. Used extensively in Mexican cooking, there is no substitute. Store it in the refrigerator for up to one week with the stems in a glass of water; cover the leaves with a plastic bag.

Jícama: A root vegetable with thin tan-brown skin and crisp, sweetish, white flesh. Shaped like a large turnip, jícama is most often used raw in salads or eaten as a refreshing snack. It should be peeled before using. Store it in the refrigerator for up to five days.

Masa Harina: A specially prepared flour used to make corn tortillas, tamales and other corn-based doughs. It is commonly available in 5-pound bags.

Mexican Chocolate: A mixture of chocolate, almonds, sugar and sometimes cinnamon and vanilla, ground together and formed into octagonal tablets. It is used in desserts, frothy chocolate beverages and, in small amounts, to add a subtle flavor enrichment to some mole sauces.

Onions: White onions with a sharp bite are used in Mexican cooking and are necessary for flavor balance and authenticity. Yellow onions are too mild and impart an undesirable sweetness when cooked.

Queso Chihuahua: A rich semi-soft cheese with a creamy color, mild flavor and good melting qualities. Mild Cheddar, Monterey Jack or Muenster can be used as substitutes.

Tomatillo (also called tomate verde or Mexican tomato): A small hard, green fruit with a papery outer husk that is pulled off before using. Tomatillos have a distinct acidic flavor and are used extensively in cooked sauces. They are available fresh or canned (often labeled tomatillo entero). There is no substitute.

Tortillas: The mainstay of Mexican cuisine. These thin, flat breads are made of corn or wheat flour. Nothing can compare with the taste and texture of freshly made tortillas, but making them at home (see recipes on pages 91 and 92) requires some practice and skill. Tortillas are readily available in the supermarket and these may be substituted for homemade tortillas. Corn tortillas usually measure between 5 and 6 inches in diameter; flour tortillas are available in many sizes, ranging from 7 to 12 inches in diameter.

CHILIES

The subject of chilies can be very confusing for beginning and experienced cooks alike. There are over 100 varieties of chilies in Mexico, each with its own unique characteristics. They are used both fresh and dried and either type can be whole or ground. The same chili can even be found under different names depending upon its region of origin. Chilies range in degree of heat from very mild to incendiary, and the heat can vary within a variety.

Due to increasing interest in Mexican foods, chilies that were once available only in Mexican grocery stores are now readily available in gourmet food stores and many local supermarkets. However, not all chilies will be available in all areas at all times. The following descriptions of the more common varieties will provide you with a basic knowledge of individual chili traits. With this knowledge, you can substitute one chili for another with similar traits. The character of the dish may change slightly, but it will still be delicious and enjoyable.

A Note of Caution: The heat of chilies comes from the seeds, the veins (the thin inner membranes to which the seeds are attached) and in the parts nearest the veins. For milder dishes, the veins and seeds are removed and discarded. The oils from the seeds and veins can be very irritating to the skin and can cause painful burning of the hands, eyes and lips. Do not touch your face while handling chilies and wash your hands well in warm soapy water after handling. Wear rubber gloves if your skin is especially sensitive or if you are handling a number of chilies.

Fresh Chilies

Fresh chilies will keep for several weeks refrigerated in a plastic bag lined with paper towels. (The towels absorb any moisture.) When purchasing fresh chilies, select those that have firm, unblemished skin.

From left to right: Anaheim, Jalapeño, Poblano and Serrano chilies

Anaheim (also called California green chili): A light green chili that has a mild flavor with a slight bite. They are 4 to 6 inches long, about 1½ inches wide and have a rounded tip. Anaheims are also sold canned. For a spicier flavor, poblano chilies can be substituted.

Jalapeño: A small, dark green chili, normally 2 to 3 inches long and about ¾ inch wide with a blunt or slightly tapered end. Their flavor varies from hot to very hot. They are also sold canned and pickled. Serranos or any other small, hot, fresh chilies can be substituted.

Poblano: A very dark green, large triangular-shaped chili with a pointed end. Poblanos are usually 3½ to 5 inches long. Their flavor ranges from mild to quite hot. For a milder flavor, Anaheims can be substituted.

Serrano: A medium green, very small chili with a very hot flavor. It usually ranges from 1 to 1½ inches in length and is about ⅜ inch wide with a pointed end. Serranos are also available pickled. Jalapeños or any other small, hot, fresh chilies can be substituted.

Dried Chilies

Dried red (ripe) chilies are usually sold in cellophane packages of various weights. They will keep indefinitely if stored in a tightly covered container in a cool, dark, dry place.

From left to right: Pasilla, Pequín, Mulato, De árbol and Ancho chilies

Ancho: A fairly large, triangular-shaped chili, slightly smaller than the mulato chili. It has wrinkled, medium to dark reddish-brown skin. Anchos are full-flavored, ranging from mild to medium-hot.

Chipotle: A smoked and dried jalapeño chili. It has wrinkled, medium-brown skin and a rich, smoky, very hot flavor. Chipotles are also commonly available canned in adobo sauce.

De árbol: A very small, slender, almost needle-shaped chili with smooth, bright red skin and a very hot flavor.

Mulato: A triangular-shaped, large chili that has wrinkled, blackish-brown skin. Its flavor is rich, pungent and medium-hot.

Pasilla: A long, slender, medium-sized chili with wrinkled, blackish-brown skin. It has a pungent flavor, ranging from mild to quite hot. (Pasillas are sometimes labeled "negro chilies.")

Pequín (also spelled piquín): A very tiny chili shaped like an oval bead. It has a slightly wrinkled, orangish-red skin. Use pequín chilies with caution as their flavor is very, very hot. (These are sometimes labeled "tepin chilies.")

HELPFUL PREPARATION TECHNIQUES

Roasting Fresh Chilies: Using tongs to hold the chili, place it directly in the medium flame of a gas burner; roast, turning as needed, until the chili is evenly blistered and charred.

Immediately place the roasted chili into a plastic bag; close the

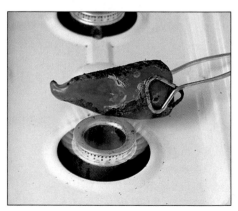

bag. Repeat with the remaining chilies. To roast in the broiler, place the chilies on a foil-lined broiler rack; roast them 2 to 3 inches from the heat until they are evenly blistered and charred, turning as needed. Place the roasted chilies in a plastic bag; close the bag.

Let the roasted chilies stand in the closed plastic bag 20 minutes. Peel each chili under cold running water, rubbing and pulling off the

charred skin. Slit the chili open lengthwise using scissors or a knife. Carefully pull out and discard the seeds and veins. Rinse the chilies well and drain; pat them dry with paper towels.

Toasting Dried Chilies: Heat an ungreased griddle or heavy skillet over medium heat; place the chilies on the griddle in a single layer. Cook the chilies 1 to 3 minutes until the color changes slightly (*but do not burn*) and the chilies become fragrant (*but not to the point of emitting a harsh aroma*), pressing them down with a spatula and turning over occasionally. If you are toasting a large number of dried chilies, place them in a single layer on a baking sheet in a 350°F oven 3 to 5 minutes until the chilies are hot to the touch and fragrant. When the chilies are cool enough to handle but still pliable, cut each one

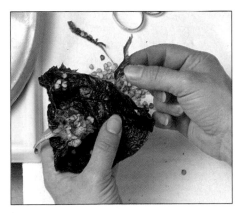

open lengthwise with scissors; carefully pull out the seeds and the veins. Only if the recipe specifies, rinse and rub chilies under cold running water.

Broiling Tomatoes: Place whole tomatoes on a foil-lined broiler rack. Broil the tomatoes 4 inches from the heat 15 to 20 minutes until the tomatoes are evenly blistered and dark brown (*not black*) on outside and soft throughout, turning as needed. Use the entire tomato; do not skin, seed or core.

Softening and Warming Tortillas: Stack the tortillas and wrap in foil. Heat the tortillas in a 350°F oven 10 minutes until the tortillas are warm. Or, warm them in a microwave oven. Stack the tortillas and wrap them in plastic wrap; microwave on HIGH ½ to 1 minute, turning them over and rotating ¼ turn once during heating.

Cheesy Chorizo Wedges

Red & Green Salsa (recipe
  follows) (optional)
8 ounces chorizo
**1 cup (4 ounces) shredded mild
  Cheddar cheese**
**1 cup (4 ounces) shredded
  Monterey Jack cheese**
**3 flour tortillas (10-inch
  diameter)**

1. Prepare Red & Green Salsa.

2. Remove and discard casing from chorizo. Heat medium skillet over high heat until hot. Reduce heat to medium. Crumble chorizo into skillet. Brown 6 to 8 minutes, stirring to separate meat. Remove with slotted spoon; drain on paper towels.

3. Preheat oven to 450°F. Mix cheeses in bowl.

4. Place tortillas on baking sheets. Divide chorizo evenly among tortillas, leaving ½ inch of edges of tortillas uncovered. Sprinkle cheese mixture over top.

5. Bake 8 to 10 minutes until edges are crisp and golden and cheese is bubbly and melted.

6. Transfer to serving plates; cut each tortilla into 6 wedges. Sprinkle Red & Green Salsa on wedges, if desired.   *Makes 6 to 8 servings*

Red & Green Salsa

1 small red bell pepper
¼ cup coarsely chopped cilantro
3 green onions, cut into thin slices
2 fresh jalapeño chilies, seeded, minced
2 tablespoons fresh lime juice
1 clove garlic, minced
¼ teaspoon salt

Cut bell pepper lengthwise in half; remove and discard seeds and veins. Cut halves lengthwise into thin slivers; cut slivers crosswise into halves. Mix all ingredients in bowl. Let stand, covered, at room temperature 1 to 2 hours to blend flavors.   *Makes 1 cup*

Step 2. Removing casing from chorizo.

Step 2. Browning chorizo.

Step 4. Sprinkling cheese mixture over tortilla.

Nachos Olé

1½ cups Refried Beans (page 90) or
    canned refried beans
  6 dozen Corn Tortilla Chips
    (page 93) or packaged corn
    tortilla chips
1½ cups (6 ounces) shredded
    Monterey Jack cheese
1½ cups (6 ounces) shredded
    Cheddar cheese
  1 large tomato
 ½ cup thinly sliced pickled
    jalapeño chilies

1. Prepare Refried Beans.

2. Prepare Corn Tortilla Chips.

3. Preheat oven to 400°F. Combine cheeses in small bowl. Reheat beans, if necessary.

4. Cut tomato crosswise in half. Gently squeeze each half to remove and discard seeds. Chop tomato.

5. Spread 1 teaspoon beans on each tortilla chip.

6. Arrange chips in single layer with edges overlapping slightly on 2 to 3 baking sheets or large ovenproof plates.

7. Sprinkle chips evenly with tomato and chilies; sprinkle with cheese mixture.

8. Bake 5 to 8 minutes until cheese is bubbly and melted. *Makes 4 to 6 servings*

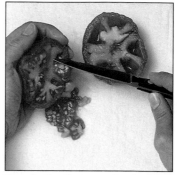

Step 4. Gently squeezing tomato half to remove seeds.

Step 5. Spreading beans on tortilla chips.

Step 7. Sprinkling chips with cheese mixture.

Cheese & Chorizo Burritos

Onion-Chili Relish* (recipe follows)
24 corn tortillas (4-inch diameter) *or* **6 flour tortillas (8-inch diameter), cut into quarters**
8 ounces queso Chihuahua or Monterey Jack cheese
4 to 6 ounces chorizo
Chilies for garnish

*Or, substitute Fresh Tomato Salsa (page 32) for the Onion-Chili Relish.

1. Prepare Onion-Chili Relish.

2. Preheat oven to 400°F. Wrap tortillas in foil.

3. Cut cheese into very thin slices. Divide slices evenly among 4 to 6 small, ovenproof plates. (Or, place slices in 1 large, shallow casserole.)

4. Remove and discard casing from chorizo. Heat medium skillet over high heat until hot. Reduce heat to medium. Crumble chorizo into skillet. Brown 6 to 8 minutes; stir to separate meat. Remove with slotted spoon; drain on paper towels. Keep warm.

5. Bake cheese 3 minutes. Place tortillas in oven; continue baking 4 minutes more or until cheese is melted.

6. Place tortillas in serving bowl; sprinkle chorizo evenly over cheese. To serve, spoon cheese mixture onto tortillas and top with relish; fold tortilla around filling. Garnish, if desired.

Makes 4 to 6 servings

Step 3. Cutting cheese into very thin slices.

Step 4. Removing casing from chorizo.

Onion-Chili Relish

1 medium white onion
1 or 2 fresh jalapeño chilies
3 tablespoons fresh lime juice
1/4 teaspoon salt

1. Cut onion and chilies lengthwise into halves. Remove and discard seeds from chilies. Cut onion and chili halves lengthwise into very thin slices; separate into slivers.

2. Combine all ingredients in bowl; mix well. Let stand, covered, at room temperature 2 hours to blend flavors. *Makes about 1 cup*

Onion-Chili Relish: Step 1. Cutting onion.

Classic Guacamole

4 tablespoons finely chopped
    white onion, divided
1½ tablespoons coarsely chopped
    cilantro, divided
1 or 2 fresh serrano or jalapeño
    chilies, seeded, finely chopped
¼ teaspoon chopped garlic
    (optional)
2 large, soft-ripe avocados
1 medium, very ripe tomato
    Boiling water
1 to 2 teaspoons fresh lime juice
¼ teaspoon salt
    Corn Tortilla Chips (page 93)
    or packaged corn tortilla
    chips
    Chilies and cilantro sprig for
    garnish

1. Combine 2 tablespoons onion, 1 tablespoon cilantro, chilies and garlic in large mortar. Grind with pestle until almost smooth. (Mixture can be processed in blender, if necessary, but it will become more watery than desired.)

2. Cut avocados lengthwise into halves; remove and discard pits. Scoop avocado flesh out of shells; place in bowl. Add chili mixture. Mash roughly with wooden spoon, bean masher or potato masher, leaving avocado slightly chunky.

3. To loosen skin from tomato, place tomato in small saucepan of boiling water 30 to 45 seconds. Rinse immediately under cold running water. Peel tomato; cut crosswise in half. Gently squeeze each half to remove and discard seeds. Chop tomato.

4. Add tomato, lime juice, salt and remaining 2 tablespoons onion and ½ tablespoon cilantro to avocado mixture; mix well. Serve immediately or cover and refrigerate up to 4 hours. Serve with Corn Tortilla Chips. Garnish, if desired.   *Makes about 2 cups*

Step 2. Scooping avocado flesh out of shells.

Step 3. Gently squeezing tomato half to remove seeds.

Step 4. Adding tomato to avocado mixture.

Mexican Tortilla Soup

6 to 8 corn tortillas (6-inch diameter), preferably day-old
2 large, very ripe tomatoes, peeled, seeded (about 1 pound) (page 16)
²/₃ cup coarsely chopped white onion
1 large clove garlic
Vegetable oil
7 cups chicken broth
4 sprigs cilantro
3 sprigs fresh mint (optional)
½ to 1 teaspoon salt
4 or 5 dried pasilla chilies
5 ounces queso Chihuahua or Monterey Jack cheese, cut into ½-inch cubes
¼ cup coarsely chopped cilantro

1. Stack tortillas; cutting through stack, cut tortillas into ½-inch-wide strips. Let strips stand, uncovered, on wire rack 1 to 2 hours to dry slightly.

2. Place tomatoes, onion and garlic in blender; process until smooth. Heat 3 tablespoons oil in large saucepan over medium heat until hot. Add tomato mixture. Cook 10 minutes, stirring frequently.

3. Add broth and cilantro sprigs to saucepan; bring to a boil over high heat. Reduce heat to low. Simmer, uncovered, 20 minutes. Add mint and salt; simmer 10 minutes more. Remove and discard cilantro and mint. Keep soup warm.

4. Heat ½ inch oil in deep, heavy, large skillet over medium-high heat to 375°F; adjust heat to maintain temperature.

5. Fry half of tortilla strips at a time, in single layer, 1 minute or until crisp, turning strips occasionally. Remove with slotted spoon; drain on paper towels.

6. Fry chilies in same oil about 30 seconds or until puffed and crisp, turning chilies occasionally. Do not burn chilies. Drain on paper towels. Cool slightly; crumble coarsely.

7. Ladle soup into bowls. Let each person add chilies, tortilla strips, cheese and chopped cilantro according to taste.

Makes 4 to 6 servings

Step 1. Cutting tortillas into ½-inch-wide strips.

Step 3. Stirring broth into tomato mixture.

Step 6. Frying chilies.

Gazpacho

6 large, very ripe tomatoes
(about 3 pounds), divided
1½ cups tomato juice
1 small clove garlic
2 tablespoons fresh lime juice
2 tablespoons olive oil
1 tablespoon white wine vinegar
1 teaspoon sugar
½ to 1 teaspoon salt
½ teaspoon dried oregano leaves,
crushed
6 green onions, cut into thin slices
¼ cup finely chopped celery
¼ cup finely chopped, seeded,
unpared cucumber
1 or 2 fresh jalapeño chilies,
seeded, minced
Garlic Croutons (recipe
follows) or packaged croutons
1 cup diced avocado
1 red or green bell pepper, seeded,
chopped
2 tablespoons cilantro
Lime wedges (optional)
Sour Cream (optional)

1. Seed and finely chop 1 tomato (page 12); set aside.

2. Coarsely chop remaining 5 tomatoes; process half of tomatoes, ¾ cup tomato juice and garlic in blender until smooth. Press through sieve into large bowl; discard seeds. Repeat with remaining coarsely chopped tomatoes and ¾ cup tomato juice.

3. Whisk lime juice, oil, vinegar, sugar, salt and oregano into tomato mixture. Stir in finely chopped tomato, onions, celery, cucumber and chilies. Cover; refrigerate at least 4 hours or up to 24 hours.

4. Prepare Garlic Croutons.

5. Stir soup; ladle into chilled bowls. Add croutons, avocado, pepper, cilantro, lime wedges and sour cream according to taste.

Makes 2 servings

Step 2. Pressing tomatoes through sieve.

Step 3. Whisking lime juice into tomato mixture.

Garlic Croutons

5 slices firm white bread
2 tablespoons olive oil
1 clove garlic, minced
¼ teaspoon paprika

1. Preheat oven to 300°F. Trim crusts from bread; cut into ½-inch cubes.

2. Heat oil in skillet over medium heat. Stir in garlic and paprika. Add bread; cook and stir 1 minute just until bread is evenly coated with oil.

3. Spread bread on baking sheet. Bake 20 to 25 minutes until crisp and golden. Cool.

Makes about 2 cups

Aztec Corn Soup

5 or 6 medium ears fresh corn*
3¹/₂ cups chicken broth
¹/₄ to ¹/₂ teaspoon salt
2 fresh poblano chilies, roasted,
  peeled, seeded, deveined
  (pages 8–9)
3 tablespoons butter or
  margarine
1 large tomato, broiled (page 9)
¹/₄ cup coarsely chopped white
  onion
¹/₂ teaspoon dried oregano leaves,
  crushed
¹/₂ cup heavy cream

*Or, substitute 2 packages (10 ounces each) frozen whole kernel corn for the fresh corn. Omit step 1. In step 2, reduce cooking time to 4 to 5 minutes.

1. Cut kernels from cobs with knife. Scrape cobs with spoon to remove pulp. Make 4 cups combined kernels and pulp.

2. Combine corn, broth and salt in 3-quart saucepan. Bring to a boil over high heat. Reduce heat to low. Cover and simmer 8 to 10 minutes until corn is tender.

3. Remove ¹/₂ cup corn from saucepan with slotted spoon; set aside. Place remaining soup, half at a time, in blender; process until smooth. Return to saucepan.

4. Cut chilies lengthwise into ¹/₂-inch-wide strips; cut strips crosswise into 2- or 3-inch lengths. Cook and stir chilies in butter in medium skillet over medium heat 4 to 5 minutes until chilies are limp and tender. Remove with slotted spoon; set aside. Reserve melted butter in skillet.

5. Place tomato, onion and oregano in blender; process until smooth. Heat reserved butter over medium heat until hot; add tomato mixture. Cook and stir 4 to 5 minutes until thickened.

6. Add tomato mixture to corn mixture in saucepan; bring to a boil over high heat. Reduce heat to low. Simmer, uncovered, 5 minutes.

7. Remove soup from heat; gradually stir in cream. Heat over very low heat 30 seconds or just until hot. *Do not boil*. Ladle into bowls. Garnish with reserved corn and chilies, if desired.   *Makes 4 to 6 servings*

Step 1. Scraping cobs with spoon to remove pulp.

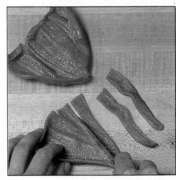

Step 4. Cutting chilies lengthwise into ¹/₂-inch-wide strips.

Step 6. Adding tomato mixture to saucepan.

Flautas with Chicken Filling

3 chicken breast halves (about
   1¹/₂ pounds)
1 can (4 ounces) diced green
   chilies, drained
¹/₂ cup water
¹/₈ teaspoon salt (optional)
¹/₂ teaspoon ground cumin
   Fresh Tomato Salsa (page 32)
1 cup Classic Guacamole
   (page 16) or prepared
   guacamole
12 corn tortillas (6-inch diameter)
   Vegetable oil
4 cups shredded iceberg lettuce
1 cup (4 ounces) shredded
   Monterey Jack cheese
¹/₂ cup sour cream
   Tomato wedges and cilantro
   sprigs for garnish

1. Combine chicken, chilies, water, salt and cumin in medium skillet. Bring to a boil over medium-high heat. Reduce heat to low. Cover; simmer 15 to 20 minutes until chicken is tender. Remove chicken; let stand until cool enough to handle. Drain chilies; reserve.

2. Prepare Fresh Tomato Salsa and Classic Guacamole.

3. Remove and discard bones and skin from chicken. With fingers, tear chicken into long, thin shreds. Warm corn tortillas (page 9).

4. For each flauta: Overlap 2 tortillas by about half of each tortilla. Spoon ¹/₈ of chicken mixture down center. Top with ¹/₈ of reserved chilies. Roll up as tightly as possible.

5. Preheat oven to 250°F. Heat 1 inch oil in deep, heavy skillet over medium-high heat to 375°F; adjust heat to maintain temperature. Line baking sheet with paper towels.

6. Fry flautas, 1 or 2 at a time, in oil, holding closed with tongs during first 30 seconds to prevent flautas from unrolling. Fry 2 minutes or until crisp and golden on all sides, turning occasionally. Drain on paper towels. Keep warm in oven on prepared baking sheet.

7. To serve, place 2 to 3 flautas on each lettuce-lined plate. Top each serving with some of the cheese, Classic Guacamole and sour cream. Garnish, if desired. Serve with Fresh Tomato Salsa.

Makes 4 to 6 servings

Step 1. Adding water to skillet.

Step 4. Forming flauta.

Step 6. Frying flautas.

Chicken Enchiladas

1 broiler-fryer chicken (about
   3 pounds), cut into 8 pieces
3 fresh poblano chilies, roasted,
   peeled, seeded, deveined, diced
   (pages 8–9)
1 large tomato, peeled, seeded,
   chopped (page 16)
1/2 cup finely chopped white onion
1 clove garlic, minced
1/2 teaspoon ground cumin
1/4 teaspoon salt
1/2 cup chicken broth
1 1/2 cups heavy cream
12 corn tortillas (6-inch diameter)
2 cups (8 ounces) shredded queso
   Chihuahua or Monterey Jack
   cheese
   Green onions and slivered red
   bell peppers for garnish
   Arroz Rojos (page 80)
   (optional)

1. Place chicken in single layer in 12-inch skillet. Sprinkle with chilies, tomato, white onion, garlic, cumin and salt; add broth. Bring to a boil over medium-high heat. Reduce heat. Cover; simmer 1 hour or until chicken is tender.

2. Remove chicken from skillet with tongs, shaking off vegetable pieces. Let stand until cool enough to handle.

3. Skim and discard fat from skillet. Bring remaining broth mixture to a boil over medium-high heat. Boil 4 to 8 minutes until mixture is reduced to 2 cups. Pour reduced broth mixture into 13 × 9-inch baking dish.

4. Remove and discard skin and bones from chicken. Using fingers, pull chicken into coarse shreds.

5. Preheat oven to 375°F. Heat cream in medium skillet over medium heat to just below boiling; remove from heat.

6. Dip 1 tortilla in cream with tongs a few seconds or until limp. Remove, draining off excess cream. Spread about 3 tablespoons chicken down center of tortilla.

7. Roll up; place on sauce in baking dish. Repeat with remaining tortillas, cream and chicken. Pour any remaining cream over enchiladas.

8. Sprinkle cheese over enchiladas. Bake 25 to 30 minutes until sauce is bubbly and cheese is melted. Garnish, if desired. Serve with Arroz Rojos. *Makes 4 to 6 servings*

Step 1. Adding broth to skillet.

Step 6. Dipping tortilla in cream.

Step 7. Forming enchilada.

Chicken Tostadas

2 cups Refried Beans (page 90) or canned refried beans
Fresh Tomato Salsa (page 32)
Lime-Cumin Dressing (recipe follows)
4 flour tortillas (10-inch diameter) *or* 8 corn tortillas (6-inch diameter)
Vegetable oil
3 cups shredded cooked chicken
4 cups shredded iceberg lettuce
1 small carrot, shredded
1 cup (4 ounces) shredded mild Cheddar cheese, divided
1 large, firm-ripe avocado, pared, pitted, sliced
1/2 cup sour cream

1. Prepare Refried Beans, mashing coarsely.

2. Prepare Fresh Tomato Salsa and Lime-Cumin Dressing.

3. Preheat oven to 250°F. Heat 1 inch oil in deep, heavy, large skillet over medium-high heat to 375°F; adjust heat to maintain temperature. Line baking sheet with paper towels.

4. Fry tortillas, 1 at a time, in oil 1 minute or until crisp and light brown, turning once. Drain on paper towels. Keep warm in oven on prepared baking sheet.

5. Reheat beans, if necessary. Combine chicken, lettuce and carrot in large bowl. Add dressing; toss to mix.

6. To serve, place 1 flour or 2 corn tortillas on each plate. Spread beans to within 1/2 inch of edge of each tortilla. Sprinkle 3/4 cup cheese evenly over tostadas. Top with chicken mixture and avocado. Garnish with remaining cheese. Serve with Fresh Tomato Salsa and sour cream. *Makes 4 servings*

Step 4. Frying tortilla.

Step 6. Sprinkling cheese over tostada.

Lime-Cumin Dressing

2 tablespoons fresh lime juice
1/4 teaspoon grated lime peel
1/4 teaspoon salt
1/4 teaspoon ground cumin
1/4 cup vegetable oil

Combine lime juice, lime peel, salt and cumin in small bowl. Gradually add oil, whisking continuously, until thoroughly blended. Store in refrigerator. *Makes about 1/3 cup*

Lime-Cumin Dressing: Whisking oil into lime juice mixture.

Beef Chimichangas

Fresh Tomato Salsa (page 32)
6 ounces chorizo
1 pound ground beef
1/2 cup finely chopped white onion
1 clove garlic, minced
1/2 teaspoon ground cumin
1 can (8 ounces) tomato sauce
1/4 cup sliced pitted ripe olives
12 flour tortillas (8-inch diameter)
1 cup (4 ounces) shredded
   Monterey Jack cheese
Vegetable oil
1 cup sour cream
   Cilantro sprigs and radishes for
   garnish

1. Prepare Fresh Tomato Salsa.

2. Remove and discard casing from chorizo. Heat large skillet over high heat until hot. Reduce heat to medium. Crumble chorizo into skillet. Brown 6 to 8 minutes, stirring to separate meat.

3. Crumble beef into skillet. Brown over medium-high heat 6 to 8 minutes, stirring to separate meat. Add onion, garlic and cumin; cook and stir 4 minutes or until onion is softened. Spoon off and discard fat.

4. Stir in tomato sauce. Bring to a boil over high heat. Reduce heat to low. Cover and simmer 15 minutes. Uncover skillet; increase heat to medium. Cook and stir 5 minutes or until most of liquid has evaporated and meat is moistly coated with sauce. Stir in olives.

5. If not freshly made, soften and warm tortillas (page 9).

6. Place 1/4 cup meat mixture on bottom half of 1 tortilla; spread to within 1 1/2 inches of bottom and side edges. Sprinkle with slightly rounded tablespoon cheese.

continued on page 32

Step 2. Removing casing from chorizo.

Step 3. Spooning off and discarding fat from skillet.

Step 4. Cooking meat mixture until most of liquid has evaporated.

Beef Chimichangas, continued

7. To form, fold bottom edge of tortilla up over filling; fold in side edges, then roll up to completely enclose filling. Secure top with wooden toothpick.

8. Repeat steps 6 and 7 with remaining tortillas, meat mixture and cheese to make 11 more chimichangas.

9. Preheat oven to 250°F. Heat 1 inch oil in deep, heavy skillet over medium-high heat to 375°F; adjust heat to maintain temperature. Line baking sheet with paper towels.

10. Fry 2 to 3 chimichangas at a time in oil 2 to 3 minutes until golden on all sides, turning occasionally. Remove with tongs; drain on paper towels. Keep warm in oven on prepared baking sheet.

11. Remove toothpicks before serving. Serve with sour cream and Fresh Tomato Salsa. Garnish, if desired.

Makes 6 servings

Fresh Tomato Salsa

1 medium tomato, finely chopped
1/4 cup coarsely chopped cilantro
2 tablespoons finely chopped white onion
1 fresh jalapeño chili, seeded, finely chopped
1 tablespoon fresh lime juice

Combine all ingredients in small bowl; mix well. Let stand, covered, at room temperature 1 to 2 hours to blend flavors. *Makes about 3/4 cup*

Step 7. Forming chimichanga.

Step 10. Frying chimichangas.

Beef Enchiladas

Red Chili Sauce (page 34)
1½ pounds lean boneless beef chuck
½ teaspoon salt
2 tablespoons vegetable oil
½ cup finely chopped white onion
¾ cup beef broth
¼ cup raisins
1 clove garlic, minced
½ teaspoon ground cloves
¼ teaspoon anise seeds, crushed
12 corn tortillas (6-inch diameter)
1 cup (4 ounces) shredded mild
   Cheddar cheese
¾ cup sour cream
⅓ cup sliced pitted ripe olives
   Basil sprig and tomato wedge
   for garnish

1. Prepare Red Chili Sauce.

2. Cut meat lengthwise with utility knife into 1-inch strips. Then cut crosswise at 1-inch intervals to form 1-inch cubes.

3. Sprinkle beef with salt. Brown half of beef in hot oil in large skillet over medium-high heat 10 to 12 minutes, turning frequently. Remove with slotted spoon to plate. Repeat with remaining beef.

4. Reduce heat to medium. Add onion; cook and stir 4 minutes or until onion is softened. Return beef to skillet. Stir in broth, raisins, garlic, cloves, anise seeds and ¼ cup Red Chili Sauce. Bring to a boil over medium-high heat. Reduce heat to low. Cover and simmer 1½ to 2 hours until beef is very tender. Using 2 forks, pull beef into coarse shreds in skillet. Remove from heat.

5. Preheat oven to 375°F. Heat remaining Red Chili Sauce in medium skillet over medium heat until hot; remove from heat.

6. Dip 1 tortilla in sauce with tongs a few seconds or until limp. Remove, draining off excess sauce.

continued on page 34

Step 3. Removing beef from skillet with slotted spoon.

Step 4. Pulling beef into coarse shreds.

Step 6. Dipping tortilla in sauce.

Beef Enchiladas, *continued*

7. Spread about 3 tablespoons meat filling down center of tortilla. Roll up; place in 13 × 9-inch baking dish. Repeat with remaining tortillas, sauce and meat filling. Pour remaining sauce over enchiladas.

8. Sprinkle cheese over top. Bake 25 minutes or until bubbly and cheese is melted. To serve, spoon sour cream down center of enchiladas. Sprinkle with olives. Garnish, if desired.

Makes 4 to 6 servings

Red Chili Sauce

3 ounces dried ancho chilies (about 5), toasted, seeded, deveined, rinsed (page 9)
2½ cups boiling water
  2 tablespoons vegetable oil
  2 tablespoons tomato paste
  1 clove garlic, minced
  ½ teaspoon salt
  ½ teaspoon dried oregano leaves, crushed
  ¼ teaspoon ground cumin
  ¼ teaspoon ground coriander

1. Place chilies in medium bowl; cover with boiling water. Let stand 1 hour.

2. Place chilies along with soaking water in blender; process until smooth.

3. Pour into 2-quart saucepan; whisk in remaining ingredients. Bring to a boil over medium-high heat. Reduce heat to very low. Cover and simmer 10 minutes, stirring occasionally.

Makes about 2½ cups

Note: Sauce can be refrigerated, covered, up to 3 days or frozen up to 1 month.

Step 7. Forming enchilada.

Red Chili Sauce: Step 1. Covering chilies with boiling water.

Red Chili Sauce: Step 3. Whisking remaining ingredients into chili mixture.

Layered Beef Enchiladas

Red Chili Sauce (page 34)
1 pound ground beef
³/₄ cup *plus* 1 tablespoon vegetable oil, divided
1 cup finely chopped white onion
1 clove garlic, minced
¹/₂ teaspoon salt
12 corn tortillas (6-inch diameter)
2 cups (8 ounces) shredded Cheddar cheese
²/₃ cup chopped pitted ripe olives
1¹/₂ cups shredded iceberg lettuce and chopped cilantro for garnish

1. Prepare Red Chili Sauce.

2. Brown beef in 1 tablespoon hot oil in large skillet over medium-high heat 6 to 8 minutes, stirring to separate meat. Add onion; cook and stir 4 minutes or until onion is softened. Spoon off and discard fat.

3. Stir garlic, salt and 1 cup Red Chili Sauce into skillet; mix well. Bring to a boil over medium heat. Reduce heat to low. Simmer, uncovered, 5 minutes or until most of liquid has evaporated and meat is moistly coated with sauce, stirring frequently.

4. Heat remaining ³/₄ cup oil in medium skillet over medium heat until hot. Fry tortillas, 1 at a time, in oil 10 to 20 seconds until just limp and blistered, turning once. Drain on paper towels. Remove and discard oil. Wipe skillet.

5. Heat remaining 1¹/₂ cups Red Chili Sauce in medium skillet over medium heat until hot.

6. Dip 1 tortilla into sauce with tongs to coat. Remove, draining off excess sauce. Place on broiler-proof individual plate. Spread about ¹/₄ cup meat filling on tortilla; sprinkle with 2 tablespoons cheese and 1 tablespoon olives. Repeat layers twice.

7. Repeat step 6 with remaining tortillas, filling, cheese and olives to make 3 more stacks. Pour any remaining sauce over enchiladas and sprinkle with remaining cheese.

8. Place enchiladas in broiler 4 inches from heat. Broil 3 minutes or until cheese is melted. Sprinkle with remaining olives. Garnish, if desired. *Makes 4 servings*

Step 2. Browning beef.

Step 4. Frying tortilla.

Step 6. Layering enchilada.

Spicy Beef Tacos

1 pound boneless beef chuck, cut
    into 1-inch cubes
    Vegetable oil
1 to 2 teaspoons chili powder
1 clove garlic, minced
$\frac{1}{2}$ teaspoon salt
$\frac{1}{2}$ teaspoon ground cumin
1 can (14$\frac{1}{2}$ ounces) whole peeled
    tomatoes, undrained, chopped
12 corn tortillas
    (6-inch diameter)*
1 cup (4 ounces) shredded mild
    Cheddar cheese
2 to 3 cups shredded iceberg
    lettuce
1 large fresh tomato, seeded,
    chopped (page 12)
    Cilantro for garnish

*Or, substitute packaged taco shells for the corn tortillas. Omit steps 4 and 5. Warm taco shells according to package directions.

1. Brown beef in 2 tablespoons hot oil in large skillet over medium-high heat 10 to 12 minutes, turning frequently. Reduce heat to low. Stir in chili powder, garlic, salt and cumin. Cook and stir 30 seconds.

2. Add undrained tomatoes. Bring to a boil over high heat. Reduce heat to low. Cover and simmer 1$\frac{1}{2}$ to 2 hours until beef is very tender.

3. Using 2 forks, pull beef into coarse shreds in skillet. Increase heat to medium. Cook, uncovered, 10 to 15 minutes until most of liquid has evaporated and beef is moistly coated with sauce. Keep warm.

4. Heat 4 to 5 inches of oil in deep fat fryer or deep saucepan over medium-high heat to 375°F; adjust heat to maintain temperature.

5. For taco shells, place 1 tortilla in taco fryer basket;** close gently. Fry tortilla $\frac{1}{2}$ to 1 minute until crisp and golden. Open basket; gently remove taco shell. Drain on paper towels. Repeat with remaining tortillas.

6. Layer beef, cheese, lettuce and tomato in each taco shell. Garnish, if desired.

Makes 6 servings

**Taco fryer baskets are available in large supermarkets and in housewares stores.

Step 1. Browning beef.

Step 3. Cooking beef until most of liquid has evaporated.

Step 5. Shaping tortilla into taco shell.

Pork Burritos

2 cups Refried Beans (page 90) or
   canned refried beans
1 boneless fresh pork butt roast
   (about 2¹/₂ pounds)
1 cup chopped white onion
1 carrot, sliced
1 clove garlic, minced
¹/₂ teaspoon salt
¹/₂ teaspoon ground cumin
¹/₂ teaspoon coriander seeds,
   lightly crushed
   Water
   Fresh Tomato Salsa (page 32)
12 flour tortillas (8-inch diameter)
2 medium, firm-ripe avocados,
   pared, pitted, diced
1 cup (4 ounces) shredded
   Monterey Jack cheese
   Carrot sticks, avocado slices
   and cilantro sprig for garnish

1. Prepare Refried Beans.

2. Place pork, white onion, sliced carrot, garlic, salt, cumin and coriander seeds in 5-quart Dutch oven. Add just enough water to cover pork. Bring to a boil over high heat. Reduce heat to low. Cover and simmer 2 to 2¹/₂ hours until pork is tender.

3. Prepare Fresh Tomato Salsa.

4. Preheat oven to 350°F. Remove pork from Dutch oven; set aside. Strain cooking liquid through cheesecloth-lined sieve; reserve ¹/₂ cup liquid.

5. Place pork on rack in roasting pan. Roast 40 to 45 minutes until well browned, turning once. Let stand until cool enough to handle.

6. Trim and discard outer fat from pork. Using 2 forks, pull pork into coarse shreds. Combine pork and reserved cooking liquid in medium skillet. Heat over medium heat 5 minutes or until meat is hot and moistly coated with liquid; stir often.

7. Soften and warm tortillas (page 9) and reheat beans, if necessary.

8. Place about 2¹/₂ tablespoons beans on bottom half of 1 tortilla; spread out slightly. Layer with pork, salsa, diced avocado and cheese.

9. To form, fold right edge of tortilla up over filling; fold bottom edge over filling, then loosely roll up, leaving left end of burrito open. Garnish, if desired.

Makes 6 servings

Step 2. Adding enough water to cover pork.

Step 6. Pulling pork into coarse shreds.

Step 9. Forming burrito.

Spicy Grilled Chicken

¹/₃ cup Chili Butter (recipe follows)
6 boneless chicken breast halves
   (about 6 ounces each)
Cilantro sprigs for garnish
Jícama-Cucumber Salad
   (page 74) (optional)
Flour Tortillas (optional)

1. Prepare Chili Butter. Cut Chili Butter into ¹/₈-inch-thick slices. Loosen skin at one end of each chicken piece; insert 1 slice of Chili Butter under skin of each piece.

2. Preheat broiler. Place chicken, skin side down, on greased rack of broiler pan; dot with some of remaining butter. Broil chicken, 6 inches from heat, 10 minutes or until tops are browned. Turn chicken over; dot with more of the remaining butter. Broil 10 minutes or until browned and juices run clear.

3. To serve, top with Chili Butter, if desired. Serve with Jícama-Cucumber Salad and tortillas. *Makes 6 servings*

Chili Butter

   1 small dried ancho chili, toasted, seeded,
      deveined, rinsed (page 9)
   1 cup boiling water
   ¹/₂ cup butter, softened
   1 clove garlic, minced
   ¹/₄ teaspoon dried oregano leaves, crushed

1. Place chili in small bowl; cover with boiling water. Let stand 1 hour.

2. Place chili and 1¹/₂ tablespoons soaking water in blender; process until smooth. Cool completely. Discard remaining soaking water.

3. Beat butter in small bowl with electric mixer until fluffy. Beat in garlic and oregano. Gradually beat in chili mixture. Cover and refrigerate 30 minutes or until firm. Spoon butter in a strip onto plastic wrap; enclose in plastic wrap and roll back and forth to form smooth 1-inch-thick roll. Refrigerate until firm. *Makes about ²/₃ cup*

Step 1. Placing Chili Butter under chicken skin.

Step 2. Dotting chicken with Chili Butter.

Chili Butter: Step 3. Rolling butter mixture into log.

Creamy Almond-Coated Chicken

½ cup blanched almonds
6 boneless skinless chicken breast
   halves (about 6 ounces each)
2 to 3 tablespoons vegetable oil,
   divided
1 tablespoon butter or margarine
¼ cup finely chopped white onion
1 fresh Anaheim or poblano chili,
   roasted, peeled, seeded,
   deveined, finely chopped
   (pages 8–9)
1 small tomato, seeded, finely
   chopped (page 12)
1 clove garlic, minced
½ cup chicken broth
¼ teaspoon salt
½ cup heavy cream
   Tomato wedge for garnish
   Cilantro sprig for garnish
   Steamed sliced summer squash
   with chopped cilantro

1. Process almonds, about ¼ at a time, with on/off pulses in electric spice grinder to fine powder. Place ground almonds on shallow plate.

2. Coat chicken with almonds; reserve remaining almonds.

3. Heat 1 tablespoon oil and butter in deep, large skillet over medium heat until foam subsides. Place breasts in single layer in skillet without crowding. Cook 6 minutes or until chicken is light brown, turning once. Reduce heat if almonds get too dark. Remove chicken to plate. Repeat with remaining chicken, adding 1 tablespoon of oil, if necessary.

4. Add remaining 1 tablespoon oil and onion to skillet. Cook and stir over medium heat 3 minutes or until onion is softened. Add chili, chopped tomato and garlic. Cook and stir 1 minute. Add broth, salt and reserved almonds. Bring to a boil over high heat.

5. Return chicken to skillet. Reduce heat to low. Cover and simmer 15 to 20 minutes until chicken is tender and juices run clear. Remove chicken to serving plate; cover and keep warm.

6. Add cream to broth mixture. Bring to a boil over medium-high heat. Cook and stir 3 to 5 minutes until sauce is slightly thickened. Pour over chicken. Garnish, if desired. Serve with summer squash. *Makes 6 servings*

Step 1. Placing ground almonds on plate.

Step 4. Cooking tomato mixture.

Step 5. Returning chicken to skillet.

Barbecued Chicken with Chili-Orange Glaze

1 or 2 dried de árbol chilies*
¹/₂ cup fresh orange juice
2 tablespoons tequila
2 cloves garlic, minced
1¹/₂ teaspoons shredded orange peel
¹/₄ teaspoon salt
¹/₄ cup vegetable oil
1 broiler-fryer chicken (about 3 pounds), cut into quarters
Orange slices and cilantro sprigs for garnish

*For milder flavor, seed some or all of the chilies.

1. Crush chilies into coarse flakes in mortar with pestle.

2. Combine chilies, orange juice, tequila, garlic, orange peel and salt in small bowl. Gradually add oil, whisking continuously, until marinade is thoroughly blended.

3. Arrange chicken in single layer in shallow glass baking dish. Pour marinade over chicken; turn pieces to coat. Marinate, covered, in refrigerator 2 to 3 hours, turning chicken over and basting with marinade several times.

4. Prepare coals for grill or preheat broiler. Drain chicken, reserving marinade. Bring marinade to a boil in small saucepan over high heat.

5. Grill or broil chicken 6 to 8 inches from heat 15 minutes, brushing frequently with marinade. Turn chicken over. Grill or broil 15 minutes more or until chicken is tender and juices run clear, brushing frequently with marinade. Garnish, if desired.

Makes 4 servings

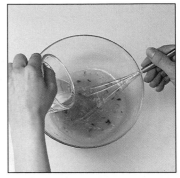
Step 2. Whisking oil into orange juice mixture.

Step 3. Basting chicken with marinade.

Step 5. Basting grilled chicken with marinade.

Chicken Mole

3 small dried pasilla chilies,
   toasted, seeded, deveined,
   rinsed (page 9)
3 small dried mulato chilies,
   toasted, seeded, deveined,
   rinsed (page 9)
1 1/2 cups boiling water
1/4 cup sesame seeds
3 whole cloves
1 piece cinnamon stick (about
   1 inch)
1/4 teaspoon whole coriander seeds
1/8 teaspoon whole anise seeds
1/4 cup vegetable oil
1/4 cup whole unblanched almonds
1/4 cup raisins
6 whole chicken legs, thighs
   attached (about 3 pounds)
1/4 teaspoon salt
1/2 cup coarsely chopped white
   onion
2 cloves garlic
1 tablespoon tomato paste
1 1/2 ounces Mexican chocolate
1 cup chicken broth
   Tomato wedges and cilantro
   sprigs for garnish
   Green Rice Pilaf (page 82)
   (optional)

1. Place pasilla and mulato chilies in medium bowl; cover with boiling water. Let stand 1 hour.

2. Toast sesame seeds in dry, heavy skillet over medium heat 2 minutes or until golden, stirring frequently. Remove from skillet.

3. Combine cloves, cinnamon stick, coriander seeds and anise seeds in same skillet; toast over medium heat 20 to 30 seconds until they start to change color and become fragrant, stirring frequently. Remove from skillet.

4. Heat oil in 12-inch skillet over medium heat until hot. Add almonds. Cook and stir 2 to 3 minutes until brown. Remove with slotted spoon; drain on paper towels.

5. Add raisins. Cook and stir 30 seconds or until puffed. Remove with slotted spoon.

6. Sprinkle chicken with salt. Cook in same skillet over medium heat 10 minutes or until browned, turning once. Remove to plate. Remove all but 2 tablespoons oil from skillet.

continued on page 50

Step 1. Covering chilies with boiling water.

Step 2. Toasting sesame seeds.

Step 4. Browning almonds.

Chicken Mole, continued

7. Place raisins in blender; process until finely ground. Coarsely chop almonds; add to blender. Process until finely ground. Add onion and garlic to blender; process until finely ground.

8. Process 2 tablespoons sesame seeds with on/off pulses in electric spice grinder to fine powder. Add to blender.

9. Process clove mixture in grinder to fine powder; add to blender.

10. Add chilies, ⅓ cup of the soaking water and the tomato paste to blender; process until smooth. If mixture is too thick, add just enough of the remaining soaking water, 1 teaspoon at a time, until blender blade can spin. Discard remaining soaking water.

11. Coarsely chop chocolate using a sharp knife.

12. Reheat oil in skillet over medium heat until hot. Reduce heat to medium-low. Add chili mixture. Cook and stir 5 minutes. Add chocolate; cook and stir 2 minutes or until melted. Gradually stir in broth. Cook and stir 5 minutes.

13. Return chicken to skillet. Reduce heat to low. Cover and simmer 45 minutes or until chicken is tender and juices run clear, turning chicken occasionally. Sprinkle remaining sesame seeds over chicken just before serving. Garnish, if desired. Serve with Green Rice Pilaf.   *Makes 6 servings*

Step 7. Adding onion to raisin mixture.

Step 10. Processed chili mixture.

Step 12. Cooking mole sauce.

Chilies Rellenos

Tomato Sauce (page 52)
8 fresh poblano or Anaheim
   chilies
Picadillo Filling (page 52)
Vegetable oil
$\frac{1}{3}$ cup all-purpose flour
5 eggs, separated
$\frac{1}{4}$ teaspoon cream of tartar
$\frac{1}{4}$ teaspoon salt
Pimiento-stuffed green olives
   for garnish

1. Prepare Tomato Sauce.

2. Roast, peel, seed and devein chilies (pages 8–9), leaving stems intact and taking care not to break chilies.

3. Prepare Picadillo Filling.

4. Carefully spoon about $\frac{1}{4}$ cup Picadillo Filling into each chili; press chilies firmly between hands to ease out air and to close.

5. Preheat oven to 250°F. Heat 1 inch oil in deep, heavy skillet over medium-high heat to 375°F; adjust heat to maintain temperature. Line baking sheet with paper towels.

6. Roll each chili in flour to coat lightly; pat off excess. Reserve remaining flour, about $\frac{1}{4}$ cup.

7. Beat egg whites, cream of tartar and salt in large bowl with electric mixer at high speed until soft peaks form. Beat egg yolks in medium bowl with electric mixer at medium speed until thick and lemon colored. Gradually beat reserved flour into egg yolks until smooth. Fold $\frac{1}{4}$ of egg whites into yolk mixture; fold in remaining egg whites until blended.

8. To coat each chili with egg batter, grasp stems; support bottom of chili with fork. Dip into batter to coat; let excess drain off.

continued on page 52

Step 4. Spooning filling into chilies.

Step 6. Rolling chili in flour.

Step 8. Coating chili with egg batter.

Chilies Rellenos, *continued*

9. Immediately slip chili into oil. Fry 4 minutes or until deep gold, turning once. Remove with slotted spatula; drain on paper towels. Keep warm in oven.

10. Reheat Tomato Sauce over medium heat. Spoon sauce on plates; arrange chilies on plates. Garnish, if desired.

Makes 4 servings

Tomato Sauce

1½ pounds tomatoes, peeled, seeded (page 16)
1 medium white onion, chopped
1 clove garlic, chopped
2 tablespoons vegetable oil
1½ cups chicken broth
 ½ teaspoon dried thyme leaves, crushed
 ¼ teaspoon salt

1. Place tomatoes, onion and garlic in blender; process until smooth.

2. Heat oil in deep, large skillet over medium heat until hot. Add tomato mixture; cook and stir 5 minutes.

3. Stir broth, thyme and salt into skillet. Bring to a boil over high heat. Reduce heat to medium-low. Cook and stir 10 to 15 minutes until sauce has thickened slightly. Remove from heat; set aside.

Makes about 2 cups

Picadillo Filling

1 tablespoon vegetable oil
¼ cup slivered almonds
¾ pound ground beef
¼ cup finely chopped white onion
1 large tomato, peeled, seeded, finely chopped (page 16)
1 tablespoon tomato paste
1 clove garlic, minced
2 tablespoons raisins
2 tablespoons thinly sliced pimiento-stuffed green olives
1 tablespoon cider vinegar
1 teaspoon dark brown sugar
¼ teaspoon salt
¼ teaspoon ground cinnamon
⅛ teaspoon ground cumin
⅛ teaspoon ground cloves

1. Heat oil in large skillet over medium heat. Add almonds; cook and stir 2 to 3 minutes until golden. Remove; drain on paper towels.

2. Crumble beef into skillet. Brown beef 5 minutes; stir often. Add onion; cook and stir 4 minutes or until softened. Add tomato, tomato paste and garlic. Cook and stir 2 minutes. Stir in remaining ingredients except almonds. Cover and simmer over low heat 15 minutes.

3. Uncover skillet; cook over medium-low 3 minutes until most of liquid has evaporated. Skim and discard fat. Stir in almonds. Let stand until cool enough to handle. *Makes about 2 cups*

Step 9. Frying chilies.

Picadillo Filling: Step 1. Toasting almonds.

Picadillo Filling: Step 2. Stirring spices into ground beef mixture.

Fajitas

2 beef skirt steaks (about 1 pound each)
2 cloves garlic, divided
3 tablespoons vegetable oil, divided
2 tablespoons *plus* 1 to 2 teaspoons fresh lime juice, divided
Dash ground black pepper
$\frac{1}{2}$ cup minced white onion
2 large tomatoes, seeded, finely chopped (page 12)
2 small green bell peppers, roasted, peeled, seeded, deveined, finely chopped (pages 8–9)
2 tablespoons minced cilantro
1 fresh serrano chili, minced
Refried Beans (page 90) (optional)
Flour Tortillas (8-inch diameter) (optional)

1. Place steaks between pieces of plastic wrap. Pound with flat side of meat mallet to $\frac{1}{4}$-inch thickness. Cut each steak crosswise into halves.

2. Pound 1 garlic clove with meat mallet to crush into coarse shreds. Combine with 2 tablespoons oil, 2 tablespoons lime juice and black pepper in large shallow glass baking dish. Add steaks, turning to coat with marinade. Marinate in refrigerator 30 minutes.

3. Mince remaining garlic clove. Cook and stir onion and garlic in remaining 1 tablespoon oil in medium skillet over medium heat 3 to 4 minutes until onion is softened. Remove from heat.

4. Stir in tomatoes, bell peppers, cilantro and chili. Season to taste with remaining lime juice. Let stand, covered, at room temperature.

5. Prepare coals for grill.* Remove steaks from marinade; pat dry with paper towels. Discard marinade. Grill 6 inches from heat 3 minutes for medium-rare or until desired doneness is reached, turning once.

6. Reheat beans, if necessary. If not freshly made, soften and warm tortillas (page 9).

7. Serve steaks with tomato relish, Refried Beans and tortillas.   *Makes 4 servings*

*Steaks can be cooked on lightly oiled, well-seasoned heavy griddle or large skillet. Heat over medium heat until very hot. Cook steaks in single layer on griddle 3 minutes for medium-rare or until desired doneness is reached, turning once.

Step 1. Pounding meat to $\frac{1}{4}$-inch thickness.

Step 4. Stirring cilantro into tomato relish.

Chili

2 tablespoons vegetable oil
2 pounds ground chuck, coarse
   chili grind or regular grind
2 cups finely chopped white
   onions
1 or 2 dried de árbol chilies
2 cloves garlic, minced
1 teaspoon ground cumin
1/2 to 1 teaspoon salt
1/4 teaspoon ground cloves
1 can (28 ounces) whole peeled
   tomatoes, undrained, coarsely
   chopped
1/2 cup fresh orange juice
1/2 cup tequila or water
1/4 cup tomato paste
1 tablespoon grated orange peel
   Lime wedges and cilantro sprigs
   for garnish

1. Heat oil in deep, 12-inch skillet over medium-high heat until hot. Crumble beef into skillet. Brown beef 6 to 8 minutes, stirring to separate meat. Reduce heat to medium. Add onions. Cook and stir 5 minutes until onions are softened.

2. Crush chilies into fine flakes in mortar with pestle. Add chilies, garlic, cumin, salt and cloves to skillet. Cook and stir 30 seconds.

3. Stir in tomatoes, orange juice, tequila, tomato paste and orange peel. Bring to a boil over high heat. Reduce heat to low. Cover and simmer 1 1/2 hours, stirring occasionally.

4. Uncover skillet. Cook chili over medium-low heat 10 to 15 minutes until thickened slightly, stirring frequently. Ladle into bowls. Garnish, if desired.   *Makes 6 to 8 servings*

Step 1. Browning ground beef.

Step 2. Crushing chilies in mortar with pestle.

Step 3. Stirring orange peel into tomato mixture.

Grilled Chili-Marinated Pork

3 tablespoons ground seeded
   dried pasilla chilies
1 teaspoon coarse or Kosher salt
$\frac{1}{2}$ teaspoon ground cumin
2 tablespoons vegetable oil
1 tablespoon fresh lime juice
3 cloves garlic, minced
2 pounds pork tenderloin or thick
   boneless loin pork chops,
   trimmed of fat
   Shredded romaine lettuce
   (optional)
   Radishes for garnish

1. Mix chilies, salt and cumin in small bowl. Stir in oil and lime juice to make smooth paste. Stir in garlic.

2. Butterfly pork by cutting lengthwise about $\frac{2}{3}$ of the way through, leaving meat in one piece; spread meat flat.

3. Cut tenderloin crosswise into 8 equal pieces. *Do not cut chops into pieces.*

4. Place pork between pieces of plastic wrap. Pound with flat side of meat mallet to $\frac{1}{4}$-inch thickness.

5. Spread chili paste on both sides of pork pieces to coat evenly. Place in shallow glass baking dish. Marinate, covered, in refrigerator 2 to 3 hours.

6. Prepare coals for grill or preheat broiler. Grill or broil pork 6 inches from heat 8 to 10 minutes for grilling or 6 to 7 minutes for broiling, turning once. Serve on lettuce-lined plate. Garnish, if desired.

Makes 6 to 8 servings

Step 2. Butterflying pork roast.

Step 3. Cutting pork roast into 8 equal pieces.

Step 4. Pounding meat to $\frac{1}{4}$-inch thickness.

Pork Stew

2 tablespoons vegetable oil

3 pounds lean, fresh boneless
    pork butt, cut into 1½-inch
    cubes

2 medium white onions, cut
    lengthwise into thin slices

3 cloves garlic, minced

1 teaspoon salt

1 teaspoon ground cumin

¾ teaspoon dried oregano leaves,
    crushed

1 cup fresh tomatillos, husked, *or*
    1 can (8 ounces) tomatillos,
    drained and chopped

3 or 4 fresh Anaheim chilies *or*
    1 can (4 ounces) green chilies,
    seeded, deveined, finely
    chopped

1 large tomato, peeled, coarsely
    chopped (page 16)

¼ cup cilantro

¾ cup chicken broth

2 teaspoons fresh lime juice

4 cups hot cooked white rice

½ cup toasted slivered almonds
    (page 52)

  Cilantro sprigs and radish slices
    for garnish

1. Heat oil in 5-quart Dutch oven over medium heat until hot. Brown pork, about ⅓ at a time, in single layer in hot oil 10 minutes, turning occasionally. Remove to plate. Repeat with remaining pork.

2. Remove and discard all but 2 tablespoons drippings from pan. Add onions and garlic. Cook and stir 4 minutes or until onions are soft. Stir in salt, cumin and oregano.

3. Add tomatillos, chilies, tomato and cilantro. Stir in broth. Bring to a boil over high heat.

4. Return pork to pan. Reduce heat to low. Cover and simmer 1½ to 2 hours until pork is tender.

5. Uncover pan. Increase heat to medium. Cook at a low boil 20 to 30 minutes until sauce is thickened, stirring occasionally. Stir in lime juice.

6. Serve pork stew over rice; sprinkle with almonds. Garnish, if desired.

Makes 10 to 12 servings

Step 1. Browning pork.

Step 2. Cooking onions.

Step 3. Stirring broth into vegetable mixture.

Spareribs Simmered in Orange Sauce

1 can (16 ounces) whole peeled
    tomatoes, undrained
2 cloves garlic
2 tablespoons vegetable oil
4 pounds country-style pork
    spareribs, cut into individual
    riblets
2 medium white onions, cut
    lengthwise into $1/4$-inch-wide
    slivers
1 to 2 tablespoons finely chopped
    seeded dried ancho chilies
$1/2$ teaspoon ground cinnamon
$1/4$ teaspoon ground cloves
$1/2$ cup fresh orange juice
$1/3$ cup dry white wine
$1/4$ cup packed dark brown sugar
1 teaspoon shredded orange peel
$1/2$ teaspoon salt
1 to 2 tablespoons cider vinegar
    Orange slices, cut into halves,
    and cilantro sprigs for garnish
$1 1/2$ pounds cooked baby carrots
    (optional)

1. Place tomatoes and garlic in blender; process until smooth. Set aside.

2. Heat oil in 5-quart Dutch oven over medium heat until hot. Brown ribs in single layer in hot oil 15 to 20 minutes, turning occasionally. Remove to plate. Repeat with remaining ribs.

3. Remove and discard all but 2 tablespoons drippings from pan. Add onions. Cook and stir 4 minutes or until onions are softened.

4. Add chilies, cinnamon and cloves to pan. Cook and stir 30 seconds. Add tomato mixture. Cook and stir 5 minutes.

5. Add orange juice, wine, brown sugar, orange peel and salt to pan. Bring to a boil over high heat. Add ribs. Reduce heat to low. Cover and simmer $1 1/2$ hours or until ribs are tender.

6. Remove ribs to plates. Skim and discard fat from liquid. Stir in vinegar; serve over ribs. Garnish, if desired. Serve with carrots.

Makes 4 to 6 servings

Step 2. Browning ribs.

Step 4. Cooking tomato mixture.

Step 5. Adding ribs to sauce.

Red Snapper in Chili-Tomato Sauce

6 red snapper fillets (8 to
  10 ounces each)
¼ teaspoon salt
⅛ teaspoon pepper
⅓ cup all-purpose flour
¼ cup olive oil
  3 cloves garlic, sliced
  2 medium white onions, cut
    lengthwise into thin slivers
1½ pounds fresh plum tomatoes,
    peeled, seeded, finely chopped
    (page 16)
½ cup tomato juice
¼ cup fresh lime juice
¼ cup sliced pimiento-stuffed
    green olives
1 or 2 pickled jalapeño chilies,
    seeded, finely chopped
1 tablespoon drained capers
1 bay leaf
  Fresh bay leaves and lime slices
    for garnish
  Boiled, quartered new potatoes
    with fresh dill (optional)

1. Sprinkle fish with salt and pepper. Coat both sides of fish with flour; shake off excess.

2. Heat oil in 12-inch skillet over medium heat. Add garlic; cook and stir 2 to 3 minutes until golden. Remove garlic with slotted spoon; discard.

3. Place fillets in single layer in skillet without crowding. Cook over medium heat 4 minutes or until fillets are light brown, turning once. Remove to plate. Repeat with remaining fillets.

4. Add onions. Cook and stir 4 minutes or until onions are softened. Stir in tomatoes, tomato juice, lime juice, olives, chilies, capers and bay leaf. Bring to a boil over high heat. Reduce heat to low. Cover and simmer 15 minutes.

5. Add any accumulated juices from fillets on plate to skillet. Increase heat to medium-high. Cook, uncovered, 2 to 3 minutes until thickened, stirring frequently. Remove and discard bay leaf.

6. Return fillets to skillet. Spoon sauce over fillets. Reduce heat to low. Cover; simmer 3 to 5 minutes until fillets flake easily when tested with a fork. Garnish, if desired. Serve with potatoes. *Makes 6 servings*

Step 1. Coating fish with flour.

Step 2. Removing garlic from skillet.

Step 4. Stirring in remaining sauce ingredients.

Fillets with Mole Verde

1/4 cup vegetable oil, divided
1/4 cup chopped white onion
1 or 2 fresh jalapeño chilies, seeded, finely chopped
1 cup fresh tomatillos, husked, *or* 1 can (8 ounces) tomatillos, drained and chopped
2 cloves garlic, minced
1/4 teaspoon ground cumin
1/3 cup *plus* 1 tablespoon water, divided
1/3 cup coarsely chopped cilantro
1/2 teaspoon salt, divided
1/3 cup all-purpose flour
1/8 teaspoon pepper
1 egg
2 tablespoons butter or margarine
1 1/2 to 2 pounds small red snapper fillets or skinless sole fillets
Cilantro sprig and tomatillos for garnish
Carrot sticks (optional)

1. Heat 2 tablespoons oil in small skillet over medium heat until hot. Add onion and chilies. Cook and stir 4 minutes or until softened. Add tomatillos, garlic and cumin. Cook and stir 1 minute.

2. Add 1/3 cup water, chopped cilantro and 1/4 teaspoon salt. Bring to a boil over high heat. Reduce heat to low. Cover and simmer 20 minutes. Pour into blender; process until smooth. Return sauce to skillet; remove from heat. Set aside.

3. Combine flour, remaining 1/4 teaspoon salt and pepper on plate. Beat egg with remaining 1 tablespoon water in shallow bowl.

4. Heat butter and remaining 2 tablespoons oil in 12-inch skillet over medium-high heat until foamy. Working with as many fillets as will fit in skillet in single layer, lightly coat each fillet on both sides with flour mixture; shake off excess. Dip into egg mixture; let excess drain off. Cook 4 to 8 minutes until light brown on outside and opaque in center, turning once. Remove to serving plate; keep warm. Repeat with remaining fillets.

5. Quickly heat reserved sauce over medium heat until hot, stirring frequently. Pour over and around fish. Garnish, if desired. Serve with carrot sticks.   *Makes 4 to 6 servings*

Step 1. Cooking tomatillos.

Step 2. Returning puréed sauce to skillet.

Step 4. Dipping fillets into egg mixture.

Baked Fish Steaks

1 tablespoon annatto seeds
1 cup boiling water
1½ tablespoons orange juice
1½ tablespoons cider vinegar
2 cloves garlic, chopped
1 small dried de árbol chili,
    coarsely crumbled
¾ teaspoon ground cumin
½ teaspoon ground allspice
¼ teaspoon salt
⅛ teaspoon pepper
4 pieces fresh halibut steaks or
    mackerel or sea bass fillets
    (about 8 ounces each)
    Vegetable oil
    Sliced green onions
    Orange peel for garnish

1. Place annatto seeds in small bowl; cover with boiling water. Let stand, covered, at room temperature at least 8 hours or overnight.

2. Drain annatto seeds; discard liquid. Place annatto seeds, orange juice, vinegar, garlic, chili, cumin, allspice, salt and pepper in blender; process until smooth.

3. Spread annatto paste over both sides of fish to coat. Arrange fish in single layer in well-oiled baking dish. Cover and refrigerate 1 to 2 hours to blend flavors.

4. Preheat oven to 350°F. Bake fish, uncovered, 20 to 25 minutes until fish flakes easily when tested with fork. Sprinkle green onions over tops before serving. Garnish, if desired. *Makes 4 servings*

Step. 1 Covering annatto seeds with boiling water.

Step 2. Adding annatto paste ingredients to blender.

Step 3. Arranging fish in baking dish.

Baked Shrimp with Chili-Garlic Butter

1½ pounds medium raw shrimp in shells
½ cup butter
¼ cup vegetable oil
8 cloves garlic, finely chopped
1 to 3 dried de árbol chilies, coarsely crumbled*
1 tablespoon fresh lime juice
¼ teaspoon salt
   Green onion tops, slivered, for garnish

*For milder flavor, seed some or all of the chilies.

1. Preheat oven to 400°F. Shell and devein shrimp, leaving tails attached; rinse and drain well.

2. Heat butter and oil in small skillet over medium heat until butter is melted and foamy. Add garlic, chilies, lime juice and salt. Cook and stir 1 minute. Remove from heat.

3. Arrange shrimp in even layer in shallow 2-quart gratin pan or baking dish. Pour hot butter mixture over shrimp.

4. Bake shrimp 10 to 12 minutes until shrimp turn pink and opaque, stirring once. Do not overcook or shrimp will be dry and tough. Garnish, if desired.   *Makes 4 servings*

Step 1. Removing shells from shrimp.

Step 2. Adding seasonings to melted butter.

Step 3. Pouring butter mixture over shrimp.

Ranchero Eggs

2 to 4 fresh serrano chilies*
1 large clove garlic
1½ pounds tomatoes, peeled, seeded (page 16)
¾ cup *plus* 2 tablespoons vegetable oil, divided
⅓ cup finely chopped white onion
¼ teaspoon salt
¼ teaspoon sugar
¼ teaspoon ground cumin
8 corn tortillas (6-inch diameter)
8 eggs
⅓ cup dry cottage cheese or farmer's cheese
1 firm-ripe avocado, pitted, pared, sliced, and cilantro sprigs for garnish

*For milder flavor, seed some or all of the chilies.

1. Place chilies and garlic in blender; process until finely chopped. Add tomatoes; process until finely chopped, but not smooth.

2. Heat 2 tablespoons oil in medium skillet over medium heat until hot. Add onion. Cook and stir 4 minutes or until onion is softened. Increase heat to medium-high. Stir in tomato mixture, salt, sugar and cumin. Cook and stir 6 to 8 minutes until sauce thickens slightly. Keep warm.

3. Preheat oven to 250°F. Line baking sheet with paper towels. Heat remaining ¾ cup oil in large skillet over medium heat until hot. Fry tortillas, 1 at a time, in oil 10 to 20 seconds until limp and blistered, turning once. Drain on paper towels. Keep warm in oven on prepared baking sheet.

4. Remove all but 2 tablespoons oil from skillet. Reduce heat to medium-low. Fry eggs, 4 at a time, 2 to 3 minutes until whites are set.

5. Arrange 2 tortillas on each plate; place 1 egg on each tortilla. Top with sauce; sprinkle with cheese. Garnish, if desired.

Makes 4 servings

Step 2. Adding puréed tomato mixture to onion mixture.

Step 3. Frying tortilla.

Step 4. Carefully adding egg to skillet to fry.

Jícama-Cucumber Salad

1 jícama (1¼ to 1½ pounds)*
1 small cucumber, unpared
½ cup very thinly slivered mild red
    onion
2 tablespoons fresh lime juice
½ teaspoon grated lime peel
1 clove garlic, minced
¼ teaspoon salt
⅛ teaspoon crumbled dried de
    árbol chili
3 tablespoons vegetable oil
    Leaf lettuce
    Red onion slivers and lime
    wedges for garnish

*Or, substitute Jerusalem artichokes. Cut pared artichokes lengthwise into halves; cut halves crosswise into thin slices.

1. Pare jícama. Cut lengthwise into 8 wedges; cut wedges crosswise into ⅛-inch-thick slices.

2. Cut cucumber lengthwise in half; scoop out and discard seeds. Cut halves crosswise into ⅛-inch-thick slices.

3. Combine jícama, cucumber and onion in large bowl; toss lightly to mix.

4. Combine lime juice, lime peel, garlic, salt and chili in small bowl. Gradually add oil, whisking continuously, until dressing is thoroughly blended.

5. Pour dressing over salad; toss lightly to coat. Cover and refrigerate 1 to 2 hours to blend flavors.

6. Serve salad in lettuce-lined salad bowl. Garnish, if desired. *Makes 6 servings*

Step 1. Cutting jícama crosswise into ⅛-inch-thick slices.

Step 2. Removing seeds from cucumber half.

Step 5. Pouring dressing over salad.

Avocados with Tomato Relish

1 tablespoon cider vinegar
1 tablespoon fresh orange juice
1 teaspoon grated orange peel
¼ teaspoon salt
    Dash pepper
3 tablespoons olive oil
3 fresh plum tomatoes (about
    ½ pound)
¼ cup coarsely chopped cilantro
2 tablespoons finely chopped mild
    red onion
1 fresh jalapeño chili, seeded,
    finely chopped
2 large, firm-ripe avocados
2 cups shredded iceberg lettuce
    Cilantro sprig, orange peel and
    tomato slice for garnish

1. Mix vinegar, orange juice, orange peel, salt and pepper in medium bowl. Gradually add oil, whisking continuously, until dressing is thoroughly blended.

2. Add tomatoes, chopped cilantro, onion and chili to dressing; toss lightly to mix. Let stand, covered, at room temperature up to 2 hours to blend flavors.

3. Just before serving, cut avocados lengthwise into halves; remove and discard pits. Pare avocados and cut lengthwise into ½-inch-thick slices.

4. Arrange avocados over lettuce-lined plates; top with tomato relish. Garnish, if desired.

Makes 4 servings

Step 1. Whisking oil into orange juice mixture.

Step 2. Adding ingredients to oil mixture to make tomato relish.

Step 3. Cutting avocados into slices.

Zesty Zucchini-Chick Pea Salad

3 medium zucchini (about
  6 ounces each)
$\frac{1}{2}$ teaspoon salt
5 tablespoons white vinegar
1 clove garlic, minced
$\frac{1}{4}$ teaspoon dried thyme leaves,
  crushed
$\frac{1}{2}$ cup olive oil
1 cup drained canned chick peas
$\frac{1}{2}$ cup sliced pitted ripe olives
3 green onions, minced
1 canned chipotle chili in adobo
  sauce, drained, seeded, minced
1 ripe avocado, pitted, pared, cut
  into $\frac{1}{2}$-inch cubes
$\frac{1}{3}$ cup crumbled feta *or* 3
  tablespoons grated Romano
  cheese
1 head Boston lettuce, cored,
  separated into leaves
  Sliced tomatoes and cilantro
  sprigs for garnish

1. Cut zucchini lengthwise into halves; cut halves crosswise into $\frac{1}{4}$-inch-thick slices. Place slices in medium bowl; sprinkle with salt. Toss to mix. Spread zucchini on several layers of paper towels. Let stand at room temperature 30 minutes to drain.

2. Combine vinegar, garlic and thyme in large bowl. Gradually add oil, whisking continuously until dressing is thoroughly blended.

3. Pat zucchini dry; add to dressing. Add chick peas, olives and onions; toss lightly to coat. Cover and refrigerate at least 30 minutes or up to 4 hours, stirring occasionally.

4. Add chili to salad just before serving. Stir gently to mix. Add avocado and cheese; toss lightly to mix.

5. Serve salad in lettuce-lined shallow bowl or plate. Garnish, if desired.

Makes 4 to 6 servings

Step 1. Draining zucchini on paper towels.

Step 2. Whisking oil into vinegar mixture.

Step 4. Adding avocado and cheese to salad.

Arroz Rojos

2 tablespoons vegetable oil
1 cup raw long-grain white rice
   (not converted)
$\frac{1}{2}$ cup finely chopped white onion
1 clove garlic, minced
$\frac{1}{2}$ teaspoon salt
$\frac{1}{2}$ teaspoon ground cumin
   Dash chili powder
2 large tomatoes, peeled, seeded,
   chopped (page 16)
1$\frac{1}{2}$ cups chicken broth
$\frac{1}{3}$ cup shelled fresh or thawed
   frozen peas
2 tablespoons chopped pimiento
   Red pepper arrows for garnish*

*To make red pepper arrows, cut a
$\frac{1}{2}$-inch-wide strip from a red pepper.
Make a V-shaped cut in strip at 1-inch
intervals.

1. Heat oil in medium skillet over medium heat until hot. Add rice. Cook and stir 2 minutes or until rice turns opaque.

2. Add onion; cook and stir 1 minute. Stir in garlic, salt, cumin and chili powder. Add tomatoes; cook and stir 2 minutes.

3. Stir in broth. Bring to a boil over high heat. Reduce heat to low. Cover and simmer 15 minutes or until rice is almost tender.

4. Stir in peas and chopped pimiento. Cover and cook 2 to 4 minutes until rice is tender and all liquid has been absorbed. Rice grains will be slightly firm and separate, rather than soft and sticky. Garnish, if desired.

Makes 4 to 6 servings

Step 1. Cooking rice until it turns opaque.

Step 2. Cooking tomatoes in rice mixture.

Step 4. Adding remaining ingredients to rice mixture.

Green Rice Pilaf

2 tablespoons vegetable oil
1 cup raw long-grain white rice
(not converted)
¹/₄ cup finely chopped white onion
2 fresh poblano or Anaheim
chilies, roasted, peeled,
seeded, deveined, chopped
(pages 8–9)
6 thin green onions, thinly sliced
1 clove garlic, minced
¹/₄ teaspoon salt
¹/₄ teaspoon ground cumin
1³/₄ cups chicken broth
1¹/₂ cups shredded queso Chihuahua
or Monterey Jack cheese
¹/₃ cup coarsely chopped cilantro
Cilantro sprig for garnish

1. Preheat oven to 375°F. Heat oil in large skillet over medium heat until hot. Add rice. Cook and stir 2 minutes or until rice turns opaque.

2. Add white onion; cook and stir 1 minute. Stir in chilies, green onions, garlic, salt and cumin; cook and stir 20 seconds.

3. Stir in broth. Bring to a boil over high heat. Reduce heat to low. Cover and simmer 15 minutes or until rice is almost tender.*

4. Remove skillet from heat. Add 1 cup cheese and chopped cilantro; toss lightly to mix. Transfer to greased 1¹/₂-quart baking dish; top with remaining ¹/₂ cup cheese.

5. Bake, uncovered, 15 minutes or until rice is tender and cheese topping is melted. Garnish, if desired.   *Makes 4 to 6 servings*

*For plain green rice, complete recipe from this point as follows: Cook rice in skillet 2 to 4 minutes more until tender. Stir in chopped cilantro just before serving; omit cheese.

Step 2. Stirring chilies, onions and seasonings into rice mixture.

Step 3. Mixing broth into rice mixture.

Step 4. Tossing cheese with rice mixture.

ON THE SIDE   83

Caramel Flan

1 cup sugar, divided
2 cups half-and-half
1 cup milk
1½ teaspoons vanilla extract
6 eggs
2 egg yolks
   Hot water
   Fresh whole and sliced
     strawberries for garnish

1. Preheat oven to 325°F. Heat 5½- to 6-cup ring mold in oven 10 minutes or until hot.

2. Heat ½ cup sugar in heavy, medium skillet over medium-high heat 5 to 8 minutes or until sugar is completely melted and deep amber color, stirring frequently. *Do not allow sugar to burn.*

3. Immediately pour caramelized sugar into ring mold. Holding mold with potholder, quickly rotate to coat bottom and sides evenly with sugar. Place mold on wire rack. (**Caution:** Caramelized sugar is very hot; do not touch it.)

4. Combine half-and-half and milk in heavy 2-quart saucepan. Heat over medium heat until almost simmering; remove from heat. Add remaining ½ cup sugar and vanilla, stirring until sugar is dissolved.

5. Lightly beat eggs and egg yolks in large bowl until blended but not foamy; gradually stir in milk mixture. Pour custard into ring mold.

6. Place mold in large baking pan; pour hot water into baking pan to depth of ½ inch. Bake 35 to 40 minutes until knife inserted into center of custard comes out clean.

7. Remove mold from water bath; place on wire rack. Let stand 30 minutes. Cover and refrigerate 1½ to 2 hours until thoroughly chilled.

8. To serve, loosen inner and outer edges of flan with tip of small knife. Cover mold with rimmed serving plate; invert and lift off mold. Garnish, if desired. Spoon some of the melted caramel over each serving.

Makes 6 to 8 servings

Step 2. Melting sugar in skillet.

Step 3. Coating mold with hot caramelized sugar.

Step 6. Inserting knife to test for doneness.

Mexican Fritters

1 cup water
¹/₂ cup butter or margarine
¹/₃ cup *plus* 1 teaspoon sugar, divided
¹/₄ teaspoon salt
¹/₄ teaspoon ground nutmeg
1 cup all-purpose flour
4 eggs
¹/₂ teaspoon vanilla extract
Vegetable oil

1. Combine water, butter, 1 teaspoon sugar, salt and nutmeg in 2-quart saucepan. Heat over medium-high heat until butter is melted, stirring occasionally. Increase heat to high. Bring to a full rolling boil.

2. Add flour all at once to saucepan; remove from heat. Beat with wooden spoon until mixture forms smooth, thick paste. Cook and stir over medium-high heat 1 to 2 minutes until mixture pulls away from side of pan and forms a ball and a film forms on bottom of pan.

3. Add eggs, 1 at a time, beating vigorously after each addition until dough is smooth and shiny. Stir in vanilla. Let dough stand at room temperature 15 minutes.

4. Heat 1 inch oil in deep, heavy, large skillet over medium-high heat to 375°F; adjust heat to maintain temperature. Line baking sheet with paper towels.

5. Spoon dough into pastry bag or cookie press fitted with large star tip (about ¹/₂ inch).

6. Carefully press dough directly into hot oil in 6-inch-long strips, cutting strips with scissors to detach. Fry strips, 3 or 4 at a time, 5 to 7 minutes until brown, turning once. Gently remove with tongs or slotted spoon; drain well on paper towels. Repeat until all dough has been fried.

7. Roll warm strips in remaining ¹/₃ cup sugar to coat lightly.   *Makes about 18 strips*

Step 2. Beating flour into butter mixture until it forms a thick paste.

Step 3. Beating in eggs until dough is smooth and shiny.

Step 6. Cutting dough strips with scissors.

Chocolate-Rum Parfaits

6 to 6 1/2 ounces Mexican chocolate
1 1/2 cups heavy cream, divided
3 tablespoons golden rum (optional)
3/4 teaspoon vanilla
   Sliced almonds for garnish
   Cookies (optional)

1. Coarsely chop chocolate using a sharp knife.

2. Combine chocolate and 3 tablespoons heavy cream in top of double boiler. Heat over simmering water until smooth, stirring occasionally. Gradually stir in rum; remove from water. Let stand at room temperature 15 minutes to cool slightly.

3. Combine remaining cream and vanilla in chilled small bowl. Beat with electric mixer at low speed, then gradually increase speed until cream is stiff, but not chunky.

4. Gently fold whipped cream into cooled chocolate mixture until uniform in color. Spoon mousse into 4 individual dessert dishes. Refrigerate 2 to 3 hours until firm. Garnish, if desired. Serve with cookies.

Makes 4 servings

Step 1. Coarsely chopping chocolate.

Step 3. Beating cream and vanilla.

Step 4. Folding whipped cream into cooled chocolate.

Refried Beans

8 ounces dried red, pink or pinto beans (1¹/₃ cups)
4¹/₂ cups cold water
¹/₃ cup *plus* 1 tablespoon vegetable shortening or vegetable oil, divided
1 small white onion, sliced
1¹/₂ teaspoons salt
1 small white onion, finely chopped
1 small clove garlic, minced

1. Rinse beans thoroughly in sieve under cold running water, picking out any debris or blemished beans.

2. Place beans, water, 1 tablespoon shortening and sliced onion in 3-quart saucepan. Bring to a boil over high heat. Reduce heat to low. Cover and simmer 1¹/₂ hours or just until beans are tender, not soft.

3. Stir in salt. Cover and simmer over very low heat 30 to 45 minutes until beans are very soft. Do not drain.*

4. Heat remaining ¹/₃ cup shortening in heavy, large skillet over high heat until very hot. Add chopped onion and garlic. Reduce heat to medium. Cook and stir 4 minutes or until onion is softened.

5. Increase heat to high. Add 1 cup undrained beans. Cook and stir, mashing beans with bean or potato masher.

6. As beans begin to dry, add another 1 cup undrained beans. Cook and stir, mashing beans with bean or potato masher. Repeat until all beans and cooking liquid have been added and mixture is a coarse purée. Adjust heat as needed to prevent beans from sticking and burning. Total cooking time will be around 20 minutes.

7. Beans may be served as a side dish or used as an ingredient for another recipe.

Makes about 2 cups

*Flavor is improved if beans are prepared to this point, then refrigerated, covered, overnight before completing recipe.

Step 1. Rinsing beans.

Step 5. Mashing beans.

Step 6. Adding cooking liquid to mashed beans.

Flour Tortillas

2 cups all-purpose flour
¹/₂ teaspoon salt
¹/₄ cup vegetable shortening
¹/₂ cup warm water

1. Combine flour and salt in medium bowl. Rub shortening into flour with fingertips until mixture has fine, even texture. Stir in water until dough forms.

2. Knead dough on floured surface 2 to 3 minutes until smooth and elastic. Wrap in plastic wrap. Let stand 30 minutes at room temperature.

3. Knead dough a few times. Divide evenly into 8 pieces for 10-inch tortillas or 12 pieces for 8-inch tortillas. Shape pieces into balls; cover with plastic wrap to prevent them from drying out.

4. Using rolling pin, roll out each dough ball on floured surface, turning over frequently, into 8- or 10-inch circle. Stack each tortilla between sheets of waxed paper.

5. Heat ungreased heavy griddle or skillet over medium-high heat until a little water sprinkled on surface dances. Carefully lay 1 tortilla on griddle; cook 20 to 30 seconds until top is bubbly and bottom is flecked with brown spots. Turn tortilla over; cook 15 to 20 seconds until flecked with brown spots. If tortilla puffs up while second side is cooking, press it down gently with spatula. Remove tortilla to foil.

6. Cook remaining tortillas as directed in step 5. If griddle becomes too hot, reduce heat to prevent burning. Stack cooked tortillas and cover with foil until all are cooked. Use immediately or wrap in foil and keep warm in 250°F oven up to 30 minutes. Tortillas are best when fresh, but can be wrapped in foil and refrigerated up to 3 days or frozen up to 2 weeks. Reheat in 350°F oven 10 minutes before using.

Makes 8 (10-inch) or 12 (8-inch) tortillas

Step 2. Kneading dough.

Step 4. Rolling dough into circle.

Step 5. Pressing tortilla down to flatten puffed area.

Corn Tortillas

2 cups masa harina
1 to 1¼ cups warm water
  Corn Tortilla Chips (page 93)

1. Cut 2 (7-inch) squares from heavy-duty plastic bag. Combine masa harina and 1 cup water in medium bowl. Add remaining water, 1 tablespoon at a time, until a smooth stiff dough is formed.

2. Test consistency of dough by rolling 1 piece dough into 1¾-inch ball; flatten slightly. Place ball on piece of plastic on lower plate of tortilla press, slightly off-center away from handle.* Cover with second piece of plastic; press down firmly with top of press to make 6-inch tortilla. Peel off top piece of plastic; invert tortilla onto hand and peel off second piece of plastic. If edges are cracked or ragged, dough is too dry; mix in water, 1 to 2 teaspoons at a time, until dough presses out with smooth edges. If tortilla sticks to plastic, dough is too wet; mix in masa harina, 1 tablespoon at a time, until dough no longer sticks when pressed.

3. When dough has correct consistency, divide evenly into 12 pieces for 6-inch tortillas or 24 pieces for 4-inch tortillas. Shape pieces into balls; cover with plastic wrap to prevent them from drying out.

4. Press out tortillas as directed in step 2, stacking between sheets of plastic wrap or waxed paper.

Step 1. Adding water, 1 tablespoon at a time, to dough.

Step 2. Flattening dough in tortilla press.

Step 2. Testing texture of flattened dough.

5. Heat ungreased heavy griddle or skillet over medium-high heat until a little water sprinkled on surface dances. Carefully lay 1 tortilla on griddle; cook 30 seconds or until edges begin to dry out. Turn tortilla over; cook 45 seconds to 1 minute until dry and lightly flecked with brown spots. Turn tortilla over again; cook first side 15 to 20 seconds more until dry and light brown. During last stage of cooking, tortilla may puff up; do not press down. Remove tortilla to kitchen towel; it will be slightly stiff, but will soften as it stands.

6. Cook remaining tortillas as directed in step 5. If griddle becomes too hot, reduce heat to prevent burning. Stack cooked tortillas and keep wrapped in towel until all are cooked. Use immediately or wrap in foil and keep warm in 250°F oven up to 30 minutes. Tortillas are best when fresh, but can be wrapped in foil and refrigerated up to 3 days or frozen up to 2 weeks. Reheat in 350°F oven 10 minutes before using.

Makes 12 (6-inch) or
24 (4-inch) tortillas

*A tortilla press works best, but if necessary, you can press with bottom of pie plate or heavy skillet.

Corn Tortilla Chips

12 corn tortillas (6-inch diameter), preferably day-old
Vegetable oil
1/2 to 1 teaspoon salt

1. If tortillas are fresh, let stand, uncovered, in single layer on wire rack 1 to 2 hours to dry slightly.

2. Stack 6 tortillas; cutting through stack, cut tortillas into 6 or 8 equal wedges. Repeat with remaining tortillas.

3. Heat 1/2 inch oil in deep, heavy, large skillet over medium-high heat to 375°F; adjust heat to maintain temperature.

4. Fry tortilla wedges in a single layer 1 minute or until crisp, turning occasionally. Remove with slotted spoon; drain on paper towels. Repeat until all chips have been fried. Sprinkle chips with salt.

Makes 6 to 8 dozen chips

Note: Tortilla chips are served with salsa as a snack, used as the base for nachos and used as scoops for guacamole, other dips or refried beans. They are best eaten fresh, but can be stored, tightly covered, in cool place 2 or 3 days. Reheat in 350°F oven a few minutes before serving.

Step 5. Cooking tortilla.

Corn Tortilla Chips: Step 2. Cutting tortillas into chips.

Corn Tortilla Chips: Step 4. Frying chips.

INDEX